Jack and the Beanstalk

First published in 2001 by
Franklin Watts
96 Leonard Street
London
EC2A 4XD

Franklin Watts Australia
56 O'Riordan Street
Alexandria
NSW 2015

A CIP catalogue record for this book is available
from the British Library.

ISBN 0 7496 4047 2 (hbk)
ISBN 0 7496 4229 7 (pbk)

Series Editor: Louise John
Series Advisor: Dr Barrie Wade
Series Designer: Jason Anscomb

Printed in Hong Kong

Jack and the Beanstalk

by Maggie Moore

Illustrated by Steve Cox

W
FRANKLIN WATTS
LONDON•SYDNEY

Once upon a time there was a boy called Jack.

Jack and his mother were very poor. All they had was a cow.

6

So, one day, Jack went to the market to sell the cow.

On the way, Jack met a little old man who wanted to buy the cow.

"I'll give you five magic beans," he told Jack.

When Jack got home,
he gave the magic beans
to his mother.

Jack's mother was very cross. She threw the beans out of the window.

During the night, the magic beans grew and grew.

By morning, a beanstalk
reached high into the sky.

Jack decided to climb the beanstalk. He climbed and climbed and when he reached the top, he found ...

... a huge castle!

Jack crept inside.

Suddenly, the floor began to shake and Jack heard a very loud voice.

"Fee, fi, fo, fum, I smell the blood of an Englishman ...

"Be he alive or be he dead, I'll grind his bones to make my bread."

It was a giant! Jack ran
into a cupboard to hide.

The giant sat down and ate a huge meal of five sheep.

Then he called for his hen.
Jack watched as the hen
laid a perfect golden egg.

The giant was full after his meal and fell fast asleep.

So, Jack crept out of the
cupboard and quickly
picked up the giant's hen.

But the hen began to
squawk and flap its wings.
The giant woke up!

"Fee, fi, fo, fum, I smell the blood of an Englishman!" he shouted.

Jack ran back to the
beanstalk and climbed
down as fast as he could.

"I'll get you!" yelled the giant as he chased Jack.

Jack reached the bottom, picked up his axe and chopped down the beanstalk.

The giant fell to the ground
with a thud.

That was the end of him!

The hen laid a golden egg
every day ...

... and Jack and his mother were never poor again.

Leapfrog has been specially designed to fit the requirements of the National Literacy Strategy. It offers real books for beginning readers by top authors and illustrators.

There are 21 Leapfrog stories to choose from:

The Bossy Cockerel
Written by Margaret Nash,
illustrated by Elisabeth Moseng

Bill's Baggy Trousers
Written by Susan Gates,
illustrated by Anni Axworthy

Mr Spotty's Potty
Written by Hilary Robinson,
illustrated by Peter Utton

Little Joe's Big Race
Written by Andy Blackford,
illustrated by Tim Archbold

The Little Star
Written by Deborah Nash,
illustrated by Richard Morgan

The Cheeky Monkey
Written by Anne Cassidy,
illustrated by Lisa Smith

Selfish Sophie
Written by Damian Kelleher,
illustrated by Georgie Birkett

Recycled!
Written by Jillian Powell,
illustrated by Amanda Wood

Felix on the Move
Written by Maeve Friel,
illustrated by Beccy Blake

Pippa and Poppa
Written by Anne Cassidy,
illustrated by Philip Norman

Jack's Party
Written by Ann Bryant,
illustrated by Claire Henley

The Best Snowman
Written by Margaret Nash,
illustrated by Jörg Saupe

Eight Enormous Elephants
Written by Penny Dolan,
illustrated by Leo Broadley

Mary and the Fairy
Written by Penny Dolan,
illustrated by Deborah Allwright

The Crying Princess
Written by Anne Cassidy,
illustrated by Colin Paine

Cinderella
Written by Barrie Wade,
illustrated by Steve Cox

The Three Little Pigs
Written by Maggie Moore,
illustrated by Rob Hefferan

The Three Billy Goats Gruff
Written by Barrie Wade,
illustrated by Nicola Evans

Goldilocks and the Three Bears
Written by Barrie Wade,
illustrated by Kristina Stephenson

Jack and the Beanstalk
Written by Maggie Moore,
illustrated by Steve Cox

Little Red Riding Hood
Written by Maggie Moore,
illustrated by Paula Knight